Table Of Contents

Getting Over Someone You've Never Dated ... 13

    Reasons Why You Can't Be With Your Crush ... 15

    It Isn't Mutual ... 17

    It's Just Physical ... 19

    When Married Or In A Relationship ... 21

    They Seem Out Of Your League ... 25

    You Don't Have The Confidence To Talk To Them ... 29

    They Are Not Good For You ... 33

    Family Or Friends Wouldn't Approve ... 37

    Crush On A Friend ... 39

    They Are A Celebrity ... 43

    They Ghosted You ... 45

Reasons You Like Them ... 51

M GORDON

It's difficult to get past a crush when you are holding on to something that you're not exactly sure of.

It's also hard to leave something or someone behind when you haven't had any closure.

Whether your crush is at school, or if they are your boss, someone you work with, or just someone you like in your community, liking someone you can't or shouldn't have can take up a huge amount of mental and emotional energy.

Initially, it can be nice to feel butterflies and warm fuzzy feelings about someone; but if that feeling becomes something that you lose command over, it can start to get tricky. If it continues, at some point, you may get to a stage where you realize you're too invested, and that your crush has more of a grip on you than you like. This can be quite difficult for your self-esteem and you may even feel a sense of rejection or embarrassment.

You may feel ashamed that you have a crush, and you may not want anyone to know that you feel this way, especially not the person that you have the crush on. Maybe you'd love to confess your feelings to the subject of your crush, but you're too shy or too scared to tell them because you think that they may not feel the same way. Or perhaps you're concerned that doing so might change the relationship in a way you don't like if they treat you differently.

When you don't feel in control, it can be scary.

This book will help you address all of these thoughts and emotions. It will also serve to help you regain control and self-confidence so you can move out of a place where you feel trapped. Regain the confidence to attract a person that is available and has mutual attributes in common with you.

We are going to cover what your crush is actually about. Establishing what's really going on to help you to overcome doubt or wishful thinking.

When you get clarity on what you REALLY want and need, it is much easier to make a new start.

This book will help you understand the psychology of what is happening to you, why you really feel what you feel, and how to break free of a crush.

Become more confident, feel more attractive and get yourself into the frame of mind where you can create the

<HOW TO GET OVER A CRUSH>

life you desire.

So let's get started.

Mia

Reasons Why You Can't Be With Your Crush

The pages in the following chapter will address some of the common reasons why a crush can't become a relationship.

We will cover obstacles for pursuing a crush, and justifications (whether moral or practical) for avoiding a scenario where you are stuck in a holding pattern you cannot escape from.

So grab a pen and paper, feel free to write notes in this book or in a journal.

It can be fascinating, satisfying even, looking back on your scribblings later on to see how you've grown at a future date.

So here goes…

It Isn't Mutual

You know the person you like doesn't feel the same about you as you think of them (sigh). You also know that the feeling isn't mutual because they have said, done, or displayed body language that indicates they are not interested in pursuing a relationship with you.

That sucks, doesn't it?

Chemistry is one thing, but the long-term sustainability of a relationship has a lot more to do with connection outside of physical chemistry. If something is off-balance, it takes a tremendous amount of energy to change what does not happen naturally.

It's a waste of energy to continually have to push your differences and insecurities down when you know you're trying to force a relationship to be what it isn't.

There are people out there that you will have great synergy with, so why waste time kidding yourself that you can make a square peg fit a round hole.

Let go now, so you can create the space for a person you have synergy with to move into.

It's Just Physical

You know that it's just a physical thing.

They are not necessarily the right person for you, and you'd never make a good couple, but you like them anyway!

I always find it interesting how someone can start off being super attracted to a person. Still, after getting to know them better, annoying traits can tend to come out of the woodwork.

The initial attraction fades as the view of the person comes into focus.

There have been many "hot" people I have met over my lifetime. Not long into getting to know them, however, their looks became secondary, and even abhorrent, due to what most people would regard as shallow or narcissistic behavior.

Just because you think someone is hot now does not mean you will feel that way when you get to know them better.

Shortcut this process, remove your rose-tinted glasses, and start paying attention to any of the traits that may annoy the heck out of you at some point.

By projecting-and injecting-a dose of reality, you could save yourself a whole lot of time in the process.

When Married Or In A Relationship

Do you like them because you can't have them, or do you like them because you admire or like who they are as a person?

Every relationship offers a few snippets of some positive or attractive traits you like or dislike. Since nobody is perfect, the person you are attracted to won't have a perfect personality or a perfect life, or a perfect relationship, for that matter, even if it appears that way.

The most likeable people are often those who are best at keeping their private life just that-private. They are also generally quite skilled at keeping their admirable, attractive traits highly visible!

It does not mean that you are seeing the true reality. It's often just what is presented to the outside world.

M GORDON

They Seem Out Of Your League

What does out of your league actually mean?

Does it mean you think someone is smarter, calmer, wittier, , prettier or more handsome, more successful, or more athletic?

The list goes on.

Is there something about them you admire, or do you wish they were more like yourself?

You may think your crush wouldn't be interested in you because you don't feel you have traits that are compatible with them.

These thoughts are often related to external appearances; they don't necessarily pertain to the soul or the personality or a person. They may have other virtues you feel but don't think about, such as integrity, honesty, or a loving, supportive nature.

I have known couples that have a seemingly harmonious relationship from the outside because they're both highly successful or sporty, for example. However, they can, at times, get very competitive with each other and forget to appreciate the opposite traits that bring balance to the relationship.

It's easy to assume someone is out of your league based entirely on outside appearances. However, this means are you making a decision for them on their behalf, without even knowing what they want.

Without knowing what they're looking for, how do you know what they want? They may be looking for something or someone entirely different for themselves.

Making assumptions on behalf of a person you haven't got to know cuts off any possibility of getting to know them in the future.

Most people want to be listened to and understood-a rare

commodity in the world of successful business people and athletes. Everyone wants to hear all about their winning game plans, but not about their struggles, even though everyone endures them.

I know several multi-millionaires who say they treasure hanging out with "real" people who aren't competing with them and who actually care about them-people who are not using them for their "toys." A genuine interest in people is a rare commodity these days. Don't underestimate your value just because you're not a [fill in the blank] person.

M GORDON

You Don't Have The Confidence To Talk To Them

Do you feel ever like you don't know what to say, or that you might not be able to speak to someone because you don't have anything in common or because you think you'll make an ass of yourself?

I know it's tough not to shut down and feel self-conscious sometimes when around your crush. You might worry about making a fool of yourself by asking the wrong question or responding to something in a way that you feel awkward about.

I've had times when I would stammer or not finish sentences because I was too concerned about what I was going to say next.

Eventually, I got over it. Now, I think about talking to

someone as an experiment, learning about who the person is, compared to whatever I thought they were like when I first saw them.

I have also learned to ask questions, pause, and wait for the answer. Allowing myself time to really contemplate what they said and what their intention was behind the statement has turned out to be an excellent antidote for nervousness when talking to people.

It doesn't really matter which walk of life you come from, whether you are from royalty or from the hood. Unless you are a member of the mafia, if you are a good listener, you will generally be valued.

When you take the spotlight off yourself, it is much easier to master the art of conversation. Another trick when somebody asks you a question is to offer a short but polite answer and consciously limit yourself to one or two sentences at most.

Again, this is a good antidote when you feel like you might start to nervously talk about yourself too much, especially if you have a habit of second-guessing yourself later.

How do you know what questions to ask?

Try to use How, What, Why, When, and Where questions as a starting point. You'll never run out of topics for conversation.

Here are a few examples: when did you arrive in this city? When did you start your new job? What kind of food do you like?

If you've recently got to know someone a little bit better, you may ask a complimentary question, such as, "Where did you get your hair color done? That color suits you."

Confidence comes from believing in yourself. And if you don't think you're good at something, you default to being a good listener.

Asking questions is a great way to find out how much somebody is interested in you without having to flirt with them to see what their level of interest is.

It's always a good starting point in any relationship or conversation.

The more in-depth the answer that you receive, the more likely the person is actually interested in you or wants to connect more.

The more you do this, the more your confidence will grow, and the more you'll develop confidence in sharing little tidbits about yourself, too.

They Are Not Good For You

You know this person is NOT someone who you have a positive future with.

Maybe they have that bad girl/bad guy thing going on, and perhaps that is exciting in contrast to feeling bored or stuck in life.

If that's the case, then visualize a future with this person-when the inevitable happens, and the cracks start to show.

What differences will become hard to tolerate later on because of your differing values?

Your inner voice should give you an indicator of what these might be, even early on.

Do you have moral differences, values which are not

aligned?

If so, it would get harder, not more comfortable, to be in a relationship, so you may as well let the "annoying" things bug you now.

Why not fast-forward the experience of the relationship to the end to help you get over it now.

<HOW TO GET OVER A CRUSH>

M GORDON

Family Or Friends Wouldn't Approve

Whether it be tradition/customs, religious reasons, or family or peer pressure, it can often be the case that you like someone that would not meet the approval of others in your world.

I have been in a relationship where my family and my partner's family had drastically different ways of doing things.

It was OK for a while (in the honeymoon period). Then, the differences became louder and a significant obstacle to the sustainability of the relationship.

Needless to say, that relationship ended.

Being brave enough to recognize and accept those differences early on can help you move past the expectations of a relationship before you get caught up in the "fantasy. Also, a small dose of "forecast reality" can save you a lot of heartaches.

Crush On A Friend

Having a crush on a friend can be torturous; you see them all the time, see their social media feeds, and watch them interacting with other people. It's tough!

What is it about the idea of a relationship with your crush that appeals to you?

Did you start to have a crush on them recently, or has it been a long-term thing?

If it is a recent development, then what has happened to push your buttons and make you see them in a different light?

Maybe you feel they fulfil a part of your world that is not being fulfilled elsewhere?

Maybe you have been hurt recently, and you feel

particularly appreciative of their support at the moment?

If it's a long-term crush, maybe that's been the case for a long time.

Are you holding back on telling them how you feel because you don't want to lose them? Or do you know they don't think that way about you?

Write down precisely what it is that they are or you think they might do that fills a void. This will give you an indication of whether it's them you like "that way," or whether it's something you can work on without them.

Some people will tell you to tell your crush how you feel. That's not a good idea, in my opinion. (Especially if they are in a relationship already), unless you have fully unpacked your reasons first.

Why?

If you discover that your reasons for having the crush were actually external, then telling them can place you or them in the following positions:

- there is a responsibility on the object-your crush-to do, feel, or say something they may prefer to avoid.

- If you later discover that they are not the "issue," it may change the relationship, and you will be less likely to have your friend to talk to about it.

Look at your crush as an opportunity to discover what you really want and need.

If you are using a person as a way to fill a void, maybe you now have more options to do so in different ways. You may even be able to do so with their support.

M GORDON

They Are A Celebrity

This one is a no-brainer and falls (obviously) under the category of fantasy. Again, use the experience as a way to uncover what you really want in your life. Then, you can plan out what you need to do to manifest what you want. Here, it is essential to focus on the opportunities and environment you want to create to attract what you want and who you want to be.

A 01
1
9
FPS
23.98
16.21.34.21
CAM
Roadside
Jakob & Ryan
Thomas Taugher

They Ghosted You

Being ghosted can bring about feelings of shame and humiliation. That hurts!

You may have been ghosted through someone's circumstances; for example, their partner doesn't want them to talk to you.

You may have been ghosted because of something you said or did, which might have been misinterpreted. This can be hard to swallow.

Whatever the case, it's essential to draw a line in the sand for yourself.

Don't go back over past mistakes or what you could have done differently-that won't change it.

Instead, focus on what you learned, and let that be a

catalyst for improvement to build confidence in what you can do differently next time.

Maybe doing something different wouldn't make a difference. Perhaps it had nothing to do with you, or there be something that is happening behind the scenes that you know nothing about.

Spending time on the negative serves you not. Instead, writing down the positives and what you can do to enhance your life can shift the negative energy you feel.

So, write down what you learned, from a positive perspective, using positive language.

What do you do that makes you feel self-respect?

What patterns can you change to feel like you are making positive change and flushing out old cobwebs?

What would you like to do and feel in your life after having the experiences you have just been through?

Are there any motivations for how you are feeling that you'd like to let go of, such as:

1. Taking things personally (e.g., being hurt by feedback someone gives you and taking it personally).

2. Self-Censorship. Being too afraid of getting bad feedback from others.

3. Not Pursuing Your Dreams. Caring what others think about your career or other choices can be debilitating.

4. People Pleasing. Wanting everyone to believe you are fantastic and approve of you, even if you don't like them! Online dating will test anyone's people-pleasing addiction.

5. "I Can Deal With This" Thinking. This is something I suffered from, without wanting to appear weak, draining, or needy. Sometimes asking for another person's perspective gives you another way to look at something and break confusion.

6. Fear of Rejection. Caring about others' opinions to the extent that you don't put yourself out there for fear of rejection is another significant reason for holding back.

7. Addiction To Approval. This is another form of

addiction. Sometimes you can like a person because they are validating, not because they are good for you.

8. Feeling Needed. It's great to feel needed and wanted, even if it's not for the right reasons. Recognizing what you're actually getting out of something can be cringeworthy, and in some cases, even downright embarrassing. Still, once you own it, you will feel a greater sense of freedom.

If any of these motivations sound familiar, or a combo of them, then you're on the way to releasing yourself from unconscious behaviors and creating new ones that serve you better.

<HOW TO GET OVER A CRUSH>

M GORDON

Reasons You Like Them

People want stuff or services for lots of different reasons. Most of the time humans are motivated by ego or security based human needs.

Writing sales copy as we know is a creative process. Like all creativity, sometimes you need some inspiration to get the creative juices going.

When looking for ways to resonate with an audiences desires and concerns you can look to some of the oldest motivators in the book - literally!

M GORDON

Projection

When you like someone, it's often because you want a picture you have created in your mind with them in it. Hence, you may be projecting a future (usually a rosy one) that is based on what you want it to be.

Like a lovey-dovey rom-com movie, you are creating a character with your crush that fits the picture you want to enjoy.

Referring back to the last page, what are you getting out of the picture you have created in your mind? What emotional fix are you trying to fulfill with the mental picture you've created.

Rather than what you want it to be, consider how much of the rosy picture you imagine is relevant to the person you have a crush on.

M GORDON

Validation & Gap FIlling

We, humans, are wired for survival and to have an identity; we have egos and a need to feel both a sense of self-worth and belonging.

We often do things or hang around people that allow us to feel validated.

I have included this section to help you identify any areas you may be trying to get validation from the idea of your crush.

We want to:

- Feel popular and included

- Feel abundant (or wealthy)

- Feel attractive

- Feel healthy

- Feel secure

- Feel peaceful and happy

- Have more time

- Have fun

Behind the desire to feel these things lies a set of human needs.

There are six basic human needs that we try, and sometimes struggle, to keep in balance. Most of these needs are unconsciously working on us in the background and manifest themselves through our programming.

We often use relationships as a mechanism to meet these needs.

The 6 Fundamental Human Needs:

1. Certainty and Security

2. Uncertainty or Variety

3. Feeling Significant or Important

4. Feeling Connected or Loved by Someone

5. Growth and Contribution

6. Contribution to the Whole (all of humanity)

1. Security. The first need to feel secure and safe is a compelling one. It is all about security and safety. The caveman genes in all of us give us the instinct to watch for predators.

2. Certainty. The second need is centered around wanting certainty, the need to know we can expect an outcome (more or less). Then, there is the exact opposite of this coin, which is the need to enjoy something different and exciting.

3. Significance. Feeling significant is another powerful driver. People want to feel they are valued and respected.

4. Connection. Feeling connected and accepted is another essential need. It's a commonly accepted fact that having a sense of belonging is vital for human growth and development. Being recognized amongst your peers makes one feel safe and happy. People will do all kinds of things to feel included.

5. Growth. People want to grow and contribute to something bigger than themselves. We have all heard stories of people who have come from humble beginnings and achieved great things. Many of us have an underlying wish to do this, if only we could muster the courage or confidence required to do so.

6. Contribution and philanthropy. This need generally applies to people who aren't living in survival mode.

The human desire to be a better person, to help others feel a sense of belonging and inclusion, is another example of contribution. We all want to be "seen" and to have the feeling we are "good."

These are some positive, motivating factors to ponder. What are you looking for in your crush that meets one or more of these needs?

<HOW TO GET OVER A CRUSH>

The Challenge

Some of us love a challenge. If someone is hard to get, we may want to prove that we can get someone's attention. Again, this is sometimes about validation rather than the actual person we think we like.

We like the chase or the feeling that we can overcome that challenge as it gives a sense of winning, and of having a sense of power, in some cases.

Sometimes rebound relationships are based on this premise. Feeling weak and jumping into another relationship is a quick, albeit temporary way of meeting a need.

Feeling good about yourself by attracting someone who gives you validation may or may not be right for you long term. The challenge of getting someone who is unattainable is a powerful draw.

More validation, or something exciting in your life?

Admiration

Admiring someone is not the same as being in love with them, even though it may feel like it. You can admire someone for something while, at the same time, truly disliking their other traits.

Admiring a strength in someone is useful for helping you to identify attributes you want to work on acquiring yourself.

Do you really like them, or do you want to aspire to be like them in some way (or ways)?

Try to separate these two things and be honest with yourself about what is motivating your admiration for your crush.

If you genuinely think someone is amazing, all you can do

is give yourself time to let your feelings pass.

You Enjoy A Good Fantasy

Some people love watching a good movie, others reading a good novel. It's fantastic to have imagination and the ability to dream. It is also lovely to be able to picture what your ideal relationship looks like. In this modern age, we see manufactured ideals on Instagram, in magazines, online, on TV (especially on so-called reality TV), and in movies.

We are surrounded by constructed realities that are designed but do not accurately depict how life really is.

Having material possessions, money, or what we think is desirable, in contrast to an authentic, unfiltered, non-photoshopped life, is like day and night.

If you accept that life is a made-up story, you can also embrace the idea that it's OK to enjoy the fantasy. You get to decide which characters are part of your story, interchange the characters, and redesign the plot.

Can you be open to the idea of having an adventure in your mind to avoid limiting yourself to one outcome?

Excitement

Excitement makes us feel alive.

We feel exhilaration from something different from our usual typical experience.

The human need for variety stands out here.

Ask yourself what questions, what excitement, you think your crush would bring to your life?

What aspects of your life do you think are boring at the moment that you'd like to make more interesting and exciting?

How do you think someone else is going to bring that to your life?

Then, you can ask the question, what am I missing in my life that makes me look at my crush and think that's what I want?

And change your internal dialogue from, "They are who I want" to "what is it that I want?"

Come up with some ideas–some experiences that you would love to have if you had the time and or money.

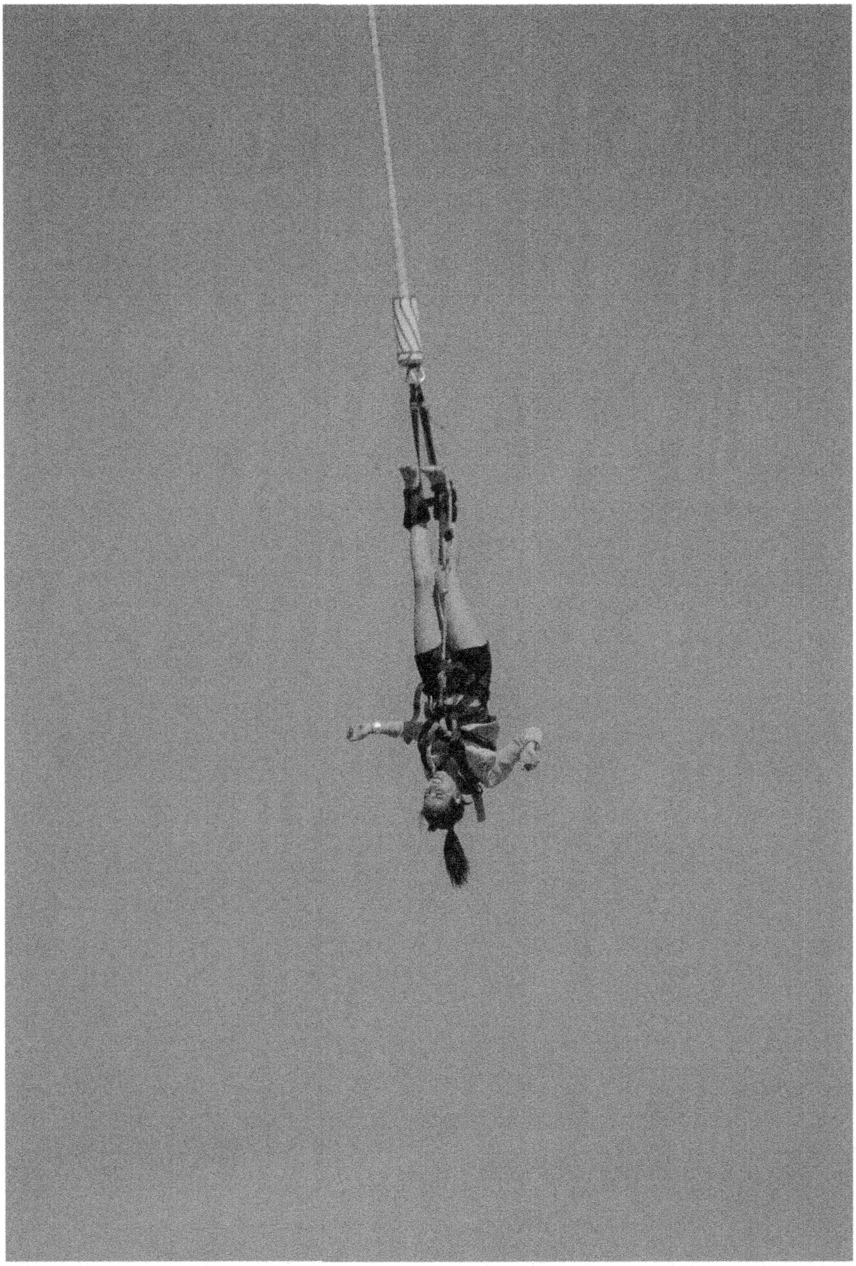

M GORDON

Contrast

If you've never experienced cold, you wouldn't know what hot felt like, right?

Are you bored or stuck in a rut and wondering what the other side of something looks and feels like?

The saying, "the grass is greener on the other side" comes to mind.

I know a lot of people who have chosen a partner because they are the opposite of themselves or an ex-partner. They were so desperate for a change, anything that got them out of the pattern they were stuck in. Like jumping on a passing bus, they chose the next someone totally different because they were a refreshing contrast to what they had been "trapped" in.

In fact, I know many people who had affairs with other

people who gave them this contrast. They were trying to escape the pain and truth about their existing relationship.

They then got stuck in the new relationship and felt they could not leave. The realization that the only reason for getting into it was out of a desperation to escape something else; it was a case of "out of the frypan into the fire."

Recognizing the contrast you are seeking before you jump means that you can make a choice that honors what you genuinely want or need.

Contrast is useful, but again, you can learn the lesson without having to go through it.

<HOW TO GET OVER A CRUSH>

M GORDON

Social Effing Media

Stories of influencers admitting to filtering and photoshopping their photos are everywhere in the news.

There are the hours and hours of prepping, filming, and editing that go into showing the world the reality influencers want people to see.

No one wants to share their imperfections online, or if they do, it is usually in a controlled manner. TMZ is not a show in which celebrities generally like their flaws being featured on.

We, mere mortals, may not have the skills to present ourselves in such a manufactured way. For some reason, we admire people who can, even when we know it's not real!

Knowing this is the case should come as a relief. We need

to remember this. It's too easy to forget that much of our reality is projected through many lenses (quite literally).

Giving yourself a break from social media is healthy to get some sanity back.

Seeing your crush online just adds to an anxiety-filled day.

F&%k Knows!

You have no idea why you like them.

After thinking about some of the theories in this book, I might have to change this statement. Sometimes, some mysteries don't need an explanation.

M GORDON

How To Stop Thinking About Someone

M GORDON

Keeping Yourself Busy

I need to cover this topic here because it can help to keep yourself busy with productive tasks or activities.

Exercise gives you an endorphin rush, while it also helps you focus on something. Moreover, starting a new activity or getting stuck into a list of things you wanted to get done or start can be invaluable.

Write a journal every time you get anxious. Let it out by writing down precisely what you feel in a safe, private place. No need to hold back here. If you are pissed off, you can let it all out here.

Do something completely different to break your usual habits. This can be hard to do when you are in mope mode, but it's worth busting through this barrier.

It feels good to have tried something new and to get out

of your comfort zone.

Write down a list of things to do and tick them off one at a time, and treat yourself for doing so.

Pattern Interrupt - Get Out Of Your Comfort Zone

Between every thought and every event in your life is a gap in which all the reactions to these events happen. How much you can extend that gap, and how much awareness you have over what happens during that gap determines the choices you have.

You can influence the outcome, and you can change your standard reaction, but only if you buy yourself time, and use a pattern interrupt.

The metaphorical toolbox you use to fix how you feel at any given time about a situation. Ask yourself whether the tools you use are actually helping you deal with the problem. You can use and even create new ones.

Do something radically different from what you usually do

when you catch yourself reacting and you may get a different result. For example, when you see your crush and get flustered, walk somewhere different, move differently, or do something entirely different from your usual practice.

Even if it's just something like eating your breakfast in a different seat. Maybe it's ordering coffee from a different store, it's important to change your habits.

On a deeper level, catch yourself thinking a thought and give yourself an alternative option or story path than you usually go down.

Change the pattern of thinking.

Change your posture. What you do with your body makes a huge difference in helping you shift your thoughts too.

Do all of these things together and watch what happens.

<HOW TO GET OVER A CRUSH>

M GORDON

Are You Being Used For Attention?

Are you being used for attention and validation?

It is flattering when someone gives you attention. Whether you like someone back or not.

Narcissistic people can be very charming, as well as damaging.

I want to cover this topic here to make sure you are not falling victim to this behavior.

What is a narcissist? Here is a definition that I found to be quite accurate: "a person who has an excessive interest in or admiration of themselves."

Narcissists LOVE to flirt and fish for compliments. They love to tell you all about THEMSELVES and THEIR issues or abilities. It's a tactic to avoid having to invest time into others (because it's all about them).

The see your "job" as making them feel good about themselves.

Narcissists feed off someone having a crush on them. Look up the traits of a narcissist and you might recognize them.

My friend spent a year dealing with one of these people. He messed with her head, enjoyed seeing her in a confused state, and set up situations where she was forced to doubt herself. He did this for fun-he got off on it!

It made me angry because I saw it all happen. He would chase her while dangling morsels for her to chase. Eventually, she escaped. Now, she looks very carefully and suspiciously at people she thinks are cute or charismatic, and recognizes when she is becoming part of their game.

Spotting these people early on can cure you of any crush you had on them.

<HOW TO GET OVER A CRUSH>

M GORDON

Language & Self Talk

Self-talk can be positive or negative. Try using language that is different to describe how you feel. Rather than saying you feel self-conscious, use reflective words.

Notice how different words make you feel differently about the thing you are thinking about. Some words, for example, invoke feelings:

ease elated courageous understanding alive content wonderful comfortable delighted blessed satisfied peaceful clever overjoyed impulsive kind ecstatic encouraged great thankful free frisky confident amazed jubilant accepting quiet important bright playful good surprised easy serene open joyous glad spirited festive certain energetic sympathetic happy animated reassured provocative calm receptive thrilled reliable pleased relaxed gleeful lucky liberated optimistic interested cheerful fortunate

admiration certain strong
interested affected fascinated
confident impulsive comforted
dynamic sensitive secure anxious
earnest warm optimistic sure
rebellious loving inspired close excited
drawn touched keen loved rosy positive attracted
challenged hardy intrigued love eager snoopy enthusiastic
brave bold intent tender
curious passionate re-enforced free
determined toward tenacious considerate
absorbed hopeful inquisitive unique
affectionate concerned engrossed
daring sympathy devoted

No Time Limit - Let Things Process

Don't give yourself a time limit to get over someone. Let yourself feel what you feel, and accept that it might take time and some mental work-though to get to the other side.

You can create new habits, as well as change your thought patterns, but be kind to yourself if it doesn't happen overnight. Write stuff down, how you feel, what you want to do, what you'd do differently, and what you will do next time.

The more you practice changing your thoughts, the easier and faster you'll get over it.

M GORDON

Journal It

Write it down if you're the type of person who likes scribbling, jotting, or doodling. Or draw pictures-let your thoughts come out. It's satisfying to look at your scribbles later on, when you've moved on, to see how far you have come and where you want to go with other areas of your life.

Those who don't like journaling may find making a video more enjoyable. You are not required to share this with anyone, so you can say what you feel.

Let it out-you can always delete it later if you wish.

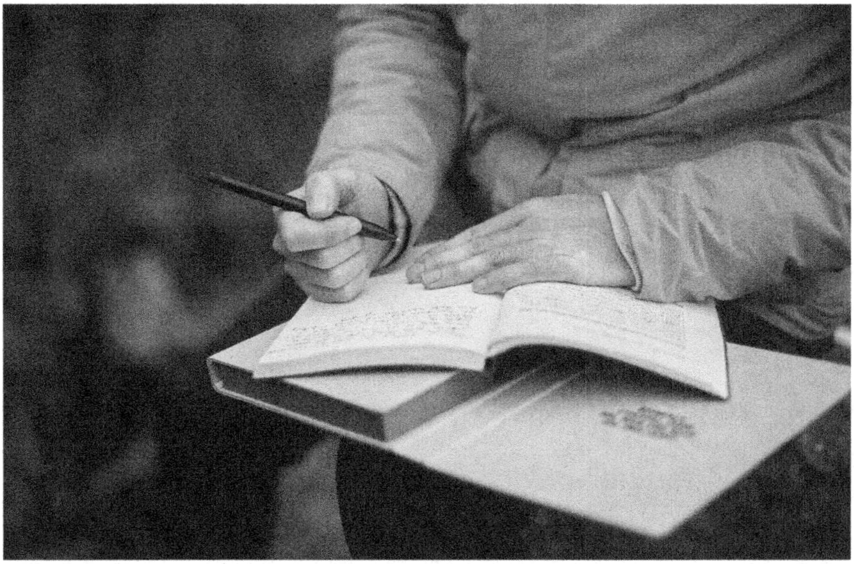

Affirmations Vs Self Torture

Be kind to yourself. Like I said earlier, don't expect to change your thought patterns in one day.

Repeating affirmations (non-verbally is fine) about what you want to create for yourself and what you are creating as you learn more about yourself helps too.

Every time you are talking yourself down, catch yourself doing so and change your language.

Change your body posture too, this can have a hugely positive effect on your state of mind also.

Write down some positive affirmations that you can read everyday to lift your energy levels.

Here are some examples:

I am the architect of my life; I build its foundation and

choose its contents.

Today, I am brimming with energy and feel content.

My body is healthy, my mind is sharp, and my soul is tranquil.

I rise above negative thoughts and actions.

I forgive those who have harmed me in my past and peacefully detach from them.

I possess the qualities needed to create the life I want.

Happiness is a choice. I base my happiness on my own accomplishments and the blessings I've been given.

My ability to conquer my challenges is limitless.

I am courageous, and I stand up for myself.

Today, I abandon my old habits and take up new, more positive ones.

Everything that is happening now is happening for my ultimate good.

<HOW TO GET OVER A CRUSH>

Though these times are difficult, they are only a short phase of life.

My future is an ideal projection of what I envision now.

I wake up today with strength in my heart and clarity in my mind.

My fears of tomorrow are simply melting away.

How To Get Over A Crush You See Every Day

If you can, keep a sensible distance so you don't have to see them every day.

Sometimes this is not possible if your crush is a friend or you see them regularly through circumstance.

If that is the case, it may help to think of something or someone else while you are in their presence, or something that grounds you.

Focus on something. Count to two with long breaths in and out, or imagine a vacation somewhere that involves something exciting or relaxing.

Stay out of clear sight of the person, if possible. If not, practice breathing in and out slowly for ten breaths. Focus on doing this to ground yourself in a more calm and peaceful state.

Practice being in the present moment rather than focusing on the past or the future.

Focus on goals, family, and other friends, plus how you can add more joy to your life by doing small things that contribute to that.

The Jerk & Silly Scenarios

If I wanted to get over being angry with someone or sad about something they did to hurt me, or even if I had a crush, I'd make up a silly character they could play the part of and imagine them playing that role.

Once I could see the ridiculous side or the funny side of what seemed to be a stupid thing they did at the time, it had become less personal.

Reframe the picture into something so that next time you see or think about someone, you will feel something different.

Draw a picture, punch something (not someone!), run, or scream-any of these things can bring amusement or relief in the moment.

M GORDON

Alternative Meanings - Change Your Picture

It is easy to tell yourself a story and put your own twist on it; be aware, your interpretation may or may not be the same as it is for someone else.

An example of this is when someone takes a long time to text you back. You can think up and imagine all kinds of reasons for the delay in replying to you.

You may be completely wrong, but it's natural to project a story filtered by your own mood or self-belief at the time.

What if you could change your story? What if you had a different range of alternative meanings you could apply to the situation?

Maybe they haven't replied to your text because their phone went flat, or they have people over visiting, and it would be rude to be on the phone. Maybe they are in a meeting.

The point here is that you can design different meanings if you choose to.

Growing Into Who Or How You Want To Be

Take all of the insights you get from looking at why you like someone and turn those into a list of things you want to grow into.

Some people like to create a dream journal or dream wall to remind them of what and who they value, as well as what and who they want to grow into and become.

Here's your opportunity to map out a journey with milestones along the way.

M GORDON

Projecting Something New - Looking Forward To The Future

Create more than one alternative picture-one that is not based around your crush. Try to come up with a few different scenarios in your mind that could be amazing for your life.

What different adventures could you go on? Where could you live? What sort of house could you live in? Where would you visit?

M GORDON

There's More Than One Person For You

There is more one person for you out there. Different people in your life bring different experiences–some may be good, while some others you might not enjoy going through. The truth is that none of us are perfect. We all have damage, and we all have different definitions of what makes us happy, which can change as time goes on.

I'm a freedom fanatic. I hate being caged, while other people love to feel secure.

I have been with people who are like or are the opposite of me. I learned from both of them.

I am now in a relationship with someone who's a bit of both, and life is pretty cool. We both love to fly helicopters, but equally enjoy snuggling up watching a movie at home.

We wouldn't appreciate each other as much as we do had we not had the previous experience of contrast with prior partners.

Claiming Your Power & Mapping Your New Picture

If you allow other people to dictate your behavior and control how you feel, you are giving your power away.

1. You are and become what you focus on.

2. What you focus on seems vivid and real because it's reflected back to you and filtered through your experiences.

3. What you focus on grows.

4. You always see and confirm in your mind what you focus on.

So, change the patterns of what you look at and what you say to yourself through self-talk.

Focus on new things and alternative realities. Project different outcomes.

Imagine them in full color, write them down, go somewhere different to where you usually go, and change your daily routine at least once a week.

How To Be Confident

M GORDON

Using Your Experiences - Making Lemonade

Every experience you go through is part of the curriculum. Much like lessons in a classroom, they are there to teach you something.

You can either waste them or extract the full value from them. Gratitude is an excellent distractor from negative thoughts and shows you how to appreciate what you get from doing something.

If you choose to look for the profit in everything, what can you extract from the experiences that teach you what you really value?

What is most important to you now that you've experienced something that isn't?

It feels good to find the value in every gift you've been

given, even if it sucked at the time.

"Don't live in the past, and don't carry the past around like a burden. Instead, use your history as one of your mentors to help refine mistakes and make changes you can invest now and the future." - **Jim Rohn**

"Most people are searching for happiness. They're looking for it. They're trying to find it in someone or something outside of themselves. That's a fundamental mistake. Happiness is something that you are, and it comes from the way you think." - **Wayne Dyer**

"If I had to live my life again, I'd make the same mistakes, only sooner." - **Tallulah Bankhead**

Write down a list of all the things you've learned, that you are glad you now know from the experiences you've had in the last few years.

What lemonade can you make from lemons?

Take a risk, make some mistakes, learn some lessons, gain some wisdom, and see where the magic takes you.

<HOW TO GET OVER A CRUSH>

Find Your Joy & Your People

Every six months, I write down a "Fuck it" list of the things I want to get over myself and do. I will also write down the things I am not going to waste my time and energy on, whether that means eliminating people or something else from my life.

I also make sure to include a "Screw it, just do it" list.

So, what do YOU want to do but haven't? Is it just a decision holding you back?

What are you good at or just love doing, or places you want to go? What would your inner superpower be?

What groups of people would you like to hang around with? Or maybe your people are animals or art?

Get rid of all the crap in your life, little by little, one day at a time, over a month. You'll be surprised how light you feel each time you do this.

Treat yourself to dreaming about something outside your comfort zone–outside what you think is possible–even if it is something small like trying a new flavor of ice cream or trying a different dish at a different place.

Give yourself permission to treat yourself to a new experience.

Recognizing Your Strengths

Write down what you are good at. What would other people say they appreciate about you? You can also write about this from your friends and family's perspective.

This can be a challenging exercise to do, which is why I am suggesting you do this from the perspective of other people around you.

Read this back to yourself.

It's not about being egotistical, it's about acknowledging your own strengths.

Just try it and see how you feel.

M GORDON

Attracting Mr or Miss Right

If you focus on something you desire, surround it with positive energy, and if you really believe it will take place, it will come into your life.

This might sound airy-fairy, but I have seen that it works!

According to the experts, manifesting the love you desire is really possible and actually quite easy.

So, here are some simple things you can do every day to manifest your perfect partner or relationship, according to experts.

1. Be Constantly Open To Opportunities

If you want the universe to work in your favor, you also need to do your part. Manifesting the love you desire actually depends on you and how open you are to getting it.

2. Keep Away From The Negativity Trap

There are some uncomplicated and pain-free methods to integrate manifestation into your everyday routine. One good way to do it is simply to try to stay positive as much as you can. Positive energy is contagious and can draw people to you. It may be difficult sometimes, but the more you practice, particularly by including positive thoughts into your day, the better you will be at it.

3. Spend 10 To 20 Minutes A Day Getting In Touch With Yourself

You can do this by writing in a journal, meditating, or standing in front of a mirror. Taking time to appreciate and know yourself makes it a lot easier to attract the healthy, positive, and long-lasting relationship that you want.

4. Be Clear About What You Really Desire In A Partner

If you want the universe to provide your perfect partner, ask yourself what your ideal partner and relationship actually looks like to you.

Trying to manifest the "perfect" person can be very challenging due to a variety of factors outside of your control. Instead, it's better to identify specific qualities or qualities that you like about the other person–it opens you up to more opportunities.

5. Wear Clothes That Make You Feel Powerful

Wear something that reflects your personality and makes you feel positive. Be aware of what you want to manifest and open to what it will look like when it gets here."

6. Do More Things That Produce Positive Vibes

Do not get stagnant. One way to do that is to keep moving forward. Keep doing things that make you feel fulfilled and pleased. "Do something that helps you develop a vibe that resonates with the type of person you would be happy with, while you're waiting on that ideal person to appear.

7. Appreciate All The Love You Currently Have In Your

Life

We've already covered how gratitude can help you feel more positive about your life and relationships. Investing a few minutes each day writing in an appreciation notebook is a straightforward method to keep you on track.

8. Remember That There's No Such Thing As Rejection

This may sound outrageous, specifically for anybody who's feeling rejection. However, think of it more as a change of state of mind. Rejection is simply the universe's way of protecting you from someone who is not an ideal fit so that you have room for somebody who is. When you no longer fear rejection, you're more most likely to attract what you really want.

Being positive all the time and having the ability to brush off rejection isn't easy. If you really believe you can manifest that relationship you want, you will.

<HOW TO GET OVER A CRUSH>

M GORDON

Conclusion

Final Words Of Advice When Writing Copy

In my plus ten years as an online marketer there are a couple of things that really stand out as the most important rules to adhere to. If I were giving advice on what you can do to make your content marketing a whole lot more effective I would say stick to quality versus quantity content.

The first thing I learned was that the amount of value I received in return for my effort was ALWAYS based on the amount of value I delivered to my audience. How much value I was able to deliver through my content was always directly rated to the amount of research I did on an audience before I started. This mean't learning what they love, hate and talk about, and most importantly how they want to FEEL through the whole process.

The second thing was to to focus on quality not quantity. Over 12 plus years I have found that writing good quality content in a slow methodical way, then placing it on websites that attract the right kind of readers is key to higher conversions. Don't bother writing content for people that aren't your target market, or are "fringe audiences". Write for websites or magazines that match your audience demographic and your results will prove to be much more effective than blasting out a series of average articles on as many sites as you can find.

Hold your head high, be stubborn about doing things well, and build your credibility in a steady manner. Don't be tempted to listen to the masses who tell you to "go hard and work your butt off" building is much content as you can. I have been there and done that as have many of my colleagues and they will all tell you - that's a great way to burn yourself out and get really sick of writing really fast.

Write for the audience you know well, devote your energy to doing a really good job for these people, the ones you know want your stuff, and they will appreciate it. So will Google and other search engines, because your visitors time on page will increase, as may your rankings. So will your conversion rates!

* * *

It's much better to start off like a tortoise, slow and steady and deliver immense value. Build a bond with your prospects. I understand that some of you will be writing for clients, and that you may be thinking this doesn't fit with your business model. From my experience and others that follow these principles, their articles convert better into longer visits onsite and greater sales, so the value of their writing services increases.

If you write posts that do more than create interest, but also build desire and deal with a lot of obstacles that the website would have to deal with otherwise, then more visitors will be preconditioned to take an action. This means less work for the website owner/webmaster to do to try and convert readers once they arrive on their website. Referrals from good articles and relevant traffic mean bounce rates go down & conversion rates often go up. Everyone wins!

So here is a summary of the general rules I follow when writing any online content. This also applies to print media, but for the benefit of the majority of readers who will be writing for websites, lets assume I am talking about online content.

Mia's top tips for online content writing:

1. Start by doing thorough homework. Spend plenty of time doing research on your audience, what are they talking about, what are their biggest wants, fears and concerns, and where are they talking about them online.

E.g. reviews, forums, social media etc.

2. Tie in their desires with the benefits of your products and services. When I say desires I don't just mean desiring a new 'widget', I mean what satisfaction will that widget deliver and how will it make them FEEL. List all the good things they might feel after purchasing it or signing up for it.

3. Don't be afraid to admit weakness and past failures as long as you explain the benefits of those failures and what you learned from them. Remember making a damaging admission tells them you aren't perfect but have learned from your mistakes, and so can they. It also infers that you are transparent and not trying to hide anything.

4. Talk about your readers concerns openly and honestly. Validate their reasons for having those concerns and then help them get past them through your processes.

5. Help your readers, serve them, give them something of value to make them feel good and more confident in what you have to offer. Demonstrated what you can do for them in small steps.

6. Bond with them and show them you are serious about helping them. Align yourself with them by talking about situations you've been that they might relate to, and share how you have overcome things they might fear but that they think they will have to get over to get what they want.

* * *

7. Clearly explain the value and appeal to their logical brain. People are emotional beings, but when it comes to handing over cash they switch into pragmatic mode. At this point they will be looking looking for excuses to justify buying something. They also want to feel like they deserve it, so give them an excuse and a reason to feel good about buying this over something else they could spend money on.

8. Add social proof such as its as examples of how the product has helped someone else, case studies or quotes by third-party sources noting the benefits of your products or services.

9. Namedrop sources of authority and any publications they have released about stats or topics that relate to what you are selling. Grow your credibility by showing you've done your homework citing facts rather than throwing in a whole lot of words just to sound authentic.

10. Explain what your reader can expect if they do what you ask them to do. Give them a clear outline of what's likely to be required of them (e.g. sign up, register, free trial). Tell them what they can expect when they click on a link and make sure what you promised is delivered at the destination you are sending them too. Use the same wording as the buttons and call to actions they are going to see when they arrive at the site you are sending them to. For example, if you are telling them they can register for something, and when they arrive at the site they see no registration button but instead a membership button

instead, they will have to stop and think "hang on, is this that I am supposed to do?". When someone arrives on a website from your content, they need to arrive and see something that makes them say to themselves "ah that's what I'm looking for". In other words don't make them work or guess what to do at the next step.

11. Create a clear and concise call to action that is explanatory e.g. *to get that do this now or before [insert time limit or number limit]*.

12. Add a summary, P.S. or reminder outlining what they can expect when they follow your call to action.

13. Remember you can also use your copy to stay in touch with your audience by inviting them to join your newsletter or ask them to follow you on social media.

That's pretty much it. That's my checklist when writing content. I like to ensure that all the articles I produce contain these elements. If I miss anything, I can generally see it in the results.

Following these principles makes for satisfying reading for your audience, they will feel like they have had a complete experience and will be preconditioned when they reach their destination because you will have done much of the work to warm them up to a purchase. You will have given them something that genuinely helps them get closer to their goal.

Don't try to be perfect, it's more important to think of

your content like a really good conversation with a new friend. If you have relayed back to a person how they feel about something, got them excited and given them something helpful and useful to them you can both feel good about the conversation.

So have fun writing and don't be shy, sign up for my monthly newsletter. Every month I go find and share latest research, tested strategies, funny stories, and lots of juicy stuff to help you write awesome content.

Come join me at http://www.mia-gordon.com, oh and you can also ask me questions if you're stuck on anything. I'll do my best to get back to you as soon as I can.

Have an awesome day and happy writing,

Final Words

The whole purpose of this book has been to shift the focus off your crush and back to your own self-awareness and empowerment.

You have all you need in your mind and body to manifest what you want in life.

Wanting something or someone is one way to spend your time. The other way is to create it by focusing on things that you can do to make what you want happen.

That doesn't have to mean wanting someone in the physical or material sense, it could mean letting go of feelings that don't serve you. It could mean saying goodbye to habits or relationships that don't fit in with what you really want.

As the author Wayne Dyer said: "Change the way you look

at things and the things you look at change."

Thanks for reading. If you enjoyed this book, please consider leaving an honest review on your favorite store.

M Gordon

Tinytodolist.com

"You yourself, as much as anybody in the entire universe, deserve your love and affection." – **Buddha**

"Until you value yourself, you won't value your time. Until you value your time, you will not do anything with it. " – **M. Scott Peck**

"What lies behind us and what lies before us are tiny matters compared to what lies within us."

– **Ralph Waldo Emerson**

<HOW TO GET OVER A CRUSH>

* * *

"When you recover or discover something that nourishes your soul and brings joy, care enough about yourself to make room for it in your life." - **Jean Shinoda Bolen**

"Self-care is never a selfish act—it is simply good stewardship of the only gift I have-the gift I was put on earth to offer to others." – **Parker Palmer**

"When you adopt the viewpoint that there is nothing that exists that is not part of you, that there is no one who exists who is not part of you, that any judgment you make is self-judgment, that any criticism you level is self-criticism, you will wisely extend to yourself an unconditional love that will be the light of the world." – **Harry Palmer**

"Owning our story and loving ourselves through that process is the bravest thing that we'll ever do." – **Brené Brown**

"One of the greatest regrets in life is being what others would want you to be, rather than being yourself." – **Shannon L. Alder**

More Wayne Dyer Quotes:

"How people treat you is their karma; how you react is yours."

"Everything is either an opportunity to grow or an obstacle to keep you from growing. You get to choose."

"When you judge another, you do not define them, you define yourself."

"You cannot always control what goes on outside. But you can always control what goes on inside."

"You are not stuck where you are unless you decide to be."

"You don't need to be better than anyone else, you just need to be better than you used to be."

"The more you see yourself as what you'd like to become, and act as if what you want is already there, the more you'll activate those dormant forces that will collaborate to transform your dream into your reality."

"I would rather be hated for who I am than loved for who I'm not."

"When you're at peace with yourself and love yourself, it is virtually impossible to do things to yourself that are destructive."

"Each experience in your life was absolutely necessary in order to have gotten you to the next place, and the next place, up to this very moment."

"I am thankful to all those who said no. It's because of them that I did it myself."

"The highest form of ignorance is when you reject

something you don't know anything about."

"There's no scarcity of opportunity to make a living at what you love. There is only a scarcity of resolve to make it happen."

"The state of your life is nothing more than a reflection of the state of your mind."

"Peace is the result of retraining your mind to process life as it is, rather than as you think it should be."

"If we focus on what's ugly, we attract more ugliness into our thoughts, and then into our emotions, and ultimately into our lives."

"It's easy to be a critic, but being a doer requires effort, risk, and change."

Remember, we are all in it together on this ~~giant~~ tiny planet!

Printed in Great Britain
by Amazon